Ea

Smoothies for Runners 2.0

24 More Proven Smoothie Recipes to Take Your
Running Performance to the Next Level, Decrease Your
Recovery Time and Allow You to Run Injury-Free

CJ Hitz

Body and Soul Publishing

COLORADO SPRINGS, COLORADO

Book Layout © 2014 BookDesignTemplates.com

Eat To Run / CJ Hitz. -- 1st ed.
ISBN-13:978-0692738450
ISBN-10:0692738452

Dedicated to my brother Jason who gave me the idea of titling this book "2.0" and continues to model the smoothie lifestyle with his daily morning blend.

Let food be thy medicine and medicine be thy food.

—HIPPOCRATES

CONTENTS

Introduction

I still love smoothies.

When I published my first *Smoothies For Runners* book back in 2012, I had no idea how it would be received. Even though I knew that nutrition was an important topic among runners and other endurance athletes, I wrote that book after seeing so many great results in my own training. I became sort of a 'mad smoothie scientist' as I threw all kinds of ingredients into my Vitamix blender before testing recipe after recipe.

It's been over 4 years since that first edition and literally thousands of people have enjoyed those 32 different recipes. And though I've specifically chosen to target runners, I've received wonderful feedback from cyclists, swimmers, walkers and even those who wouldn't consider themselves to be 'athletes.' After all, everyone can enjoy the healthy nutritional benefits of a smoothie!

In *Smoothies For Runners 2.0*, you're going to enjoy 24 more new and exciting recipes that will add some real nutritional bang for your buck. Along with a description for each recipe, I've also included a new feature where I share a "Training Tip" that correlates with the name of each smoothie. These training tips are geared toward runners but endurance athletes in other sports should be able to grasp the concept and apply each tip to their own training.

As someone who continues to compete as a national class masters runner, it's crucial that I give my body the nutrients it requires for optimal performance. At age 43 (as of June 2016), I can't get away with some of the ways I treated my body in my 20s.

Since taking up running in 2008 after nearly 20 years away from the sport, I've continued to get faster each year. I attribute much of that improvement to a better understanding of what my body needs nutritionally. Smoothies have played a significant role, especially in regard to my recovery.

I still believe that the most important part of tomorrow's run is what you do in the first 15 minutes after today's run. By consuming a smoothie with a nice combination of protein and carbohydrate, you give your body immediate building materials to utilize for recovery since the blender has done some of the work of breaking down the ingredients. Yet with a smoothie, you retain the fiber necessary for helping the body bind up and get rid of waste. This fiber also prevents a sugar rush or insulin spike that can occur with pure fruit juices. I'm certainly not opposed to juicing but I believe runners need as much fiber as they can get, especially post-run.

I also continue to believe that a true smoothie must contain at least one fruit. Otherwise, it's simply a "shake" as far as I'm concerned.

Thanks for joining me on this second smoothie adventure…let the blending begin!

Cinnamon Roll Recovery

When I was growing up, my family would take the occasional trip to Eugene, Oregon where we would visit the big indoor mall. Within that mall was a place most of us are familiar with called Cinnabon where huge, gooey cinnamon rolls were served warm. I always looked forward to that treat! This smoothie offers a cooler, healthier version to help satisfy that sweet, cinnamon craving. Cinnamon is a wonderful spice that can yield several health benefits including increased blood circulation and prevention of blood clots. The essential oils in cinnamon also help qualify it as an "anti-microbial" food which can stop the growth of bacteria and fungi. Finally, studies have shown that simply smelling cinnamon can boost cognitive function...in other words...it's great brain food!

Ingredients

1 cup unsweetened almond, coconut or rice milk

1 frozen ripe banana

1 scoop Garden of Life® RAW vanilla protein powder

¼ cup vanilla Greek yogurt or non-dairy alternative (i.e. So Delicious®)

½ tsp. cinnamon

2 ice cubes

Blend all ingredients until smooth

Nutrition Facts

350 calories, 18g protein, 74g carbohydrates

*Training Tip

As runners, we can easily develop knots or "hot spots" in our muscles as we train. To stay on top of these stubborn areas, it's important to utilize a foam roller every day to aid in recovery. Here's a link where I share more detail about using this important tool for maintenance - http://www.trainwellracewell.com/how-to-use-a-foam-roller-for-injury-prevention-in-running/

Chocaramel Almond D-Lite

Sometimes we just need to splurge and enjoy a decadent dessert. With this smoothie, you can enjoy the flavors of chocolate, caramel and almonds while also gaining some quality nutrition. Almonds are high in vitamin E and have also been shown to reduce LDL-cholesterol as much as first generation statin drugs. Almonds are a very satiating snack with 6g of protein per serving (about 22 nuts). Who knew that going nuts could be so healthy?

Ingredients
1 cup chocolate almond milk
1 frozen ripe banana
4 pitted medjool dates
1 scoop Garden of Life® Smooth Chocolate Organic Plant Protein
1 Tbsp. almond butter

¼ tsp. almond extract
Almond slices or chocolate chips for garnish

Blend all ingredients until smooth

Nutrition Facts
570 calories, 20g protein, 127 carbohydrates

*Training Tip
If you're going to splurge, whether it's a decadent smoothie or another sweet treat, you might as well earn it by clearing some hard-earned calories with a nice long run. Studies have shown longer, slower runs to be very efficient at fat burning. Many runners will differ on their definition of a long run, but I believe 90 minutes or more will begin to tap into those fat stores as fuel. Most of us will agree that food always tastes better after a long run!

CocoMint Christmas Cheer

This is a great recipe to bring out during the Christmas season with mint being a constant theme. The fresh peppermint leaves will ensure that this is technically a green smoothie. Peppermint has long been shown to be a remedy for indigestion or an upset stomach. This herb also aids in breathing (a benefit for runners) and can help relieve symptoms of colds related to allergy. Take a deep breath and enjoy!

Ingredients
1 cup vanilla or chocolate coconut milk, depending on your preference
8 fresh mint leaves
1 frozen ripe banana

1 scoop Garden of Life® Smooth Vanilla Organic Plant Protein

1-2 drops Peppermint oil extract (optional for stronger mint lovers)

Blend all ingredients until smooth

Nutrition Facts
280 calories, 16g protein, 48g carbohydrates

*Training Tip
For whatever reason (weather perhaps?), many people seem to have the idea that a good time to take it easy with training is between Thanksgiving and New Year. In my opinion, the opposite is true. Not that you have to train like a maniac during this stretch but it's a good idea to still stay consistent. There are simply too many dietary landmines at our fingertips to slack off completely. There's nothing wrong with enjoying the myriad of tasty treats that accompany the season but planning ahead can make a huge difference. So about 2-3 weeks before Thanksgiving, write out a training plan on your own, with a partner or with a coach that includes what you'll be doing each day between turkey day and January 1st. This schedule will help keep you accountable to staying actively engaged with training in the midst of one temptation after another.

Key Lime Strides

As you start sipping on this refreshing smoothie, you may start imagining yourself taking in the sunshine and warm breeze of the Florida Keys. No problem, savor the moment! Limes, like all citrus fruit, are a great source of vitamin C which supports our immune system. It's interesting to note that in several villages in West Africa where cholera epidemics occurred, the consumption of lime juice during the main meal of the day was found to protect against the contraction of cholera. The healing properties of lemons & limes have also been shown to alter or slow down cell division within the body, including cancer cells. Pucker up and enjoy!

Ingredients

1 cup plain coconut milk

1 5.3oz cup Chobani® Key Lime Greek yogurt

Juice squeezed from 1 key lime or regular lime

1 Tbsp. shredded coconut

1 graham cracker sheet

5 drops liquid stevia (careful, a little goes a long way)

Blend all ingredients until smooth

Nutrition Facts

300 calories, 14g protein, 42g carbohydrates

*Training Tip

Just like a dash of fresh lime juice can add some punch to a recipe, so can strides add a punch to your running. A stride is simply 15-20 seconds of running at mile to 5k race pace. I recommend inserting strides into one or two of your weekly easy runs, either in the middle or at the end of the run. I personally like to add five 20 second strides toward the end of an easy run while my legs are nice and warmed up. Each stride is followed by 20-30 seconds of easy jogging. Strides help keep our legs sharp and tuned for speed by activating some of the fast twitch muscle fibers. Simply put, strides will add a little zest to your running!

'Beet' Your Rivals

Fruits & vegetables with deep red or purple color are excellent sources of anthocyanins (berries) and betalain (beets). These antioxidants give our bodies an immunity boost and also have anti-inflammatory benefits. Beets have also been found to be high in nitrate which our bodies reduce to nitrite for generation of nitric oxide. Nitric Oxide (N-O) is responsible for dilation of blood vessels, blood circulation and aiding in endurance. Who can't use a little more endurance?

Ingredients

½ cup cold black cherry juice

½ cup cold beet juice (Another option I enjoy is adding beet juice powder to my smoothies. My preferred brand is BeetElite (www.BeetElite.com)

½ cup frozen wild blueberries

½ cup frozen sweet cherries

Handful of raw spinach leaves

Blend all ingredients until smooth

Nutrition Facts
210 calories, 50g carbohydrates

*Training Tip
I'm not sure about you, but I've had several rivals over the years on both the roads and trails. Rivals can motivate us to train harder which can push us to new breakthroughs in our running. I encourage you to look around and find a few people who consistently finish near or slightly ahead of you in some of the local races you run. It's perfectly fine to introduce yourself and share some mutual goals and upcoming races you're training for. Friendly rivalries can lead to some great friendships…and personal bests!

Cuconut Craving

This refreshing smoothie combines a couple of powerhouse hydrators with coconut water and cucumber. Cucumbers belong to the same botanical family as both melons and squashes which provide an ample source of vitamin K (aids blood clotting, bone health). Coconut water is an excellent source of the following electrolytes that are found in the human body: calcium, magnesium, phosphorous, potassium and sodium. These electrolytes help prevent muscle cramping which can sometimes stop us runners in our tracks.

Ingredients

1 cup cold coconut water

⅓ cucumber

1 small celery stalk

1 Tbsp. shredded coconut

½ ripe pear

Small handful raw baby spinach

Blend all ingredients until smooth

Nutrition Facts
150 calories, 28g carbohydrates, 7.5g fiber

*Training Tip
Speaking of cravings, we will naturally crave things that we feed our bodies on a regular basis. Refined sugar has been found to be one of the most addictive substances on earth, comparable to cocaine! The more we consume, the more our bodies cry out for it. The next time you get that sweet tooth, reach for an apple, orange or banana. The fiber contained in fruit helps prevent and buffer the sugar crash that inevitably follows after eating cookies, donuts or candy bars. If you can try this exchange for 3 weeks straight, you'll be on your way to "re-training" both your taste buds and your cravings.

Pineapple Plank

Pineapple is an excellent source of the trace mineral manganese which aids in the energy production that happens within our mitochondria (energy production factories within the cells). If you're feeling low on energy, just getting some fresh pineapple into your body can provide a quick boost for a run. This tropical fruit is also high in vitamin C which strengthens our immune system.

Ingredients

1 cup plain coconut milk
½ cup frozen or fresh cold pineapple
½ cup fresh chopped papaya
1 Tbsp. shredded coconut
1 5.3oz cup Chobani® Pineapple flavored Greek yogurt or non-dairy alternative (i.e. So Delicious®)

Blend all ingredients until smooth

Nutrition Facts
287 calories, 12g protein, 38g carbohydrates

*Training Tip
Planks are an incredible way to strengthen our core. As runners, we need a strong core in order to help us maintain form in the latter part of a tough race. The weaker the core, the sloppier our form which drains our bodies of energy as we call upon other muscles to pick up the slack. I like to do 1-3 minutes of planking at night before going to bed. Straight arm planks are basically a push-up in the "up" position as the arms are straight and palms of the hands on the floor. Bent arm planks are done with the forearms and elbows touching the floor and holding that position. You want your back & legs to be in a nice straight line (not a hump or slouch) while really focusing on engaging that core. In the beginning, start small and add 1-5 seconds each time. Before long, you'll not only be up to 3 minutes, but possibly 5, 10 or 15 minutes at a time! Don't forget to breathe while planking and expect some shaking to occur as you try holding good form.

Savory Splits

With this smoothie concoction, we deviate from the sweet side of things to a saltier blend of goodness. And technically this recipe does include a fruit with the avocado. Avocado is an excellent source of the "good" fats, including monounsaturated fatty acid and oleic acid which support cardiovascular health. Tomatoes contain a hefty amount of the phytonutrient lycopene which have been shown to decrease total cholesterol, LDL cholesterol and triglyceride levels in the blood. As a runner, you'll do your body a huge favor by consuming this smoothie at least once a week.

Ingredients
1 ½ cups water
1 cup romaine lettuce
1 medium tomato
½ cup chopped carrot
½ avocado
1 garlic clove
1 celery stalk
½ tsp. sea salt
Pinch of cayenne pepper
Ice cubes (optional)

Blend all ingredients until smooth

Nutrition Facts
228 calories, 23g carbohydrates, 15g fats

*Training Tip
Splits are simply your times to mile markers or kilometers within a race or a workout. Consider them checkpoints that give you key feedback along the way to the finish line. Almost every distance running world record has been set by achieving a negative split which is running the second half of the race faster than the first. It's easy to start a race by going out too hard and then fading to the finish. By monitoring your splits, you're able to adjust your pace and give yourself the chance to finish strong. Now that's a savory thought!

Blueberry Bonk

In this delicious smoothie, the mighty wild blueberry takes center stage. These little blue power pellets are full of phytonutrients that serve as anti-inflammatories for the runner. And if you've been running long enough, you know that inflammation is an enemy that slows recovery. Some new discoveries are showing blueberries to also be a cognitive aid, specifically in the area of memory. We could on and on with other benefits but you get the idea. Wild blueberries have a flavor punch that many prefer over the regular variety and they contain more nutrients pound for pound.

Ingredients
1 ½ cups vanilla flavored coconut milk
1 scoop Garden of Life® Smooth Vanilla Organic Plant Protein

1 5.3oz cup Chobani® Blueberry flavored Greek yogurt or non-dairy alternative (i.e. So Delicious®)

1 cup frozen wild blueberries

Pinch of cinnamon (optional)

Blend all ingredients until smooth

Nutrition Facts

445 calories, 59g carbohydrates, 27g protein

*Training Tip

The term 'bonking' simply refers to another phrase many of us are familiar with called 'hitting the wall.' This is when muscle glycogen stores become depleted and a feeling of fatigue hits you. To avoid the dreaded "B-word" it's important to properly fuel 2-3 hours before a longer race or training run where glycogen is crucial. In fact, getting a good portion of carbs into your body the evening before is also helpful. And it doesn't need to be the typical pasta overload that many people practice. It could be a baked white or sweet potato, yams or a good helping of wild or brown rice with roasted veggies. When you fuel good...you feel good!

Mocha Morning Warm-up

The jury is still out regarding the health benefits of coffee but some studies have indicated that moderate (2-3 8oz cups per day) consumption has been linked to a decrease in heart disease. Too much java can lead to jitters and caffeine overload. It may not sound healthy but adding the coconut oil and real butter (stay far away from margarine) adds a nice dose of healthy fats that our bodies crave. These healthy fats also provide a lubricating effect for our joints. You're going to love the smooth texture this morning energizer offers!

Ingredients

1 cup strong hot coffee

½ cup hot water

1 scoop Garden of Life® Chocolate Cacao RAW Protein

2 soaked pitted Medjool dates

1 Tbsp. coconut oil

1 Tbsp. butter or non-dairy olive oil spread

Pour over ice to cool down (optional)

Blend all ingredients until smooth

Nutrition Facts

442 calories, 43g carbohydrates, 26g fat, 18g protein, 9.2g dietary fiber

*Training Tip

Have a key race or workout coming up? A good warm-up can make a huge difference in your performance and injury prevention. I like to do a minimum of 2 miles easy running and then some dynamic stretching & drills (leg swings, high knees, skipping) in the 30-40 minutes leading up to a race. Showing up on a start line and taking off at race pace without any warm-up is like starting a car and immediately taking off after it's been sitting all night in sub-freezing temperatures. Running hard on cold muscles is a strain or tear waiting to happen. Take the extra time to warm-up...your body will thank you for it.

Strawberry Kiwi Kick

Looking for a vitamin C boost? Kiwis and strawberries offer a great 1-2 punch in this area (don't forget the lemon juice as another great source). If you're using iron as a supplement, taking it with fruits high in vitamin C will help your body absorb it more effectively. Studies have also shown that eating vitamin C-rich fruits can add a significant protective effect against respiratory issues like wheezing associated with asthma. This smoothie recipe provides a light and refreshing burst of nutrition.

Ingredients
1 cup unsweetened almond milk
1 kiwi (peeled)

½ cup frozen or fresh strawberries
½ cup So Delicious® vanilla non-dairy yogurt
1 squeezed lemon wedge or 1 tsp. lemon juice

Blend all ingredients until smooth

Nutrition Facts
157 calories, 23g carbohydrates, 6.6g fat, 8g dietary fiber

*Training Tip
Having a good finishing 'kick' can mean the difference between holding your position, passing a few other runners, or becoming the roadkill others pass in the last 200-400 meters of a race. Having enough left in the tank to finish strong is a huge confidence booster, especially if you're the predator rather than the prey. One way you can practice a finishing kick is by saving your best effort for the end of a workout. For example, if you're doing a 3 mile tempo run, finish the last 200-400 meters with an all-out burst of speed. If you're doing an 8 x 400 meter interval session on the track, reach back on that last one and try running 1-2 seconds faster than any of the previous ones.

Pumpkin Pie PR

If you're like me, you don't really get tired of pumpkin pie at Thanksgiving time. With this smoothie, you satisfy that pumpkin pie craving while still getting some great nutrition. Pumpkin (along with most squash) is an excellent source of vitamin A which aids vision, especially in dim light. This is a good thing when going out for that evening trail run. Though bananas are widely touted for their potassium content, pumpkins contain even more of this electrolyte-restoring nutrient! Consider this recipe a nice recovery "dessert" after a run.

Ingredients
1 cup vanilla almond milk
½ cup pumpkin puree
½ rozen banana
1 scoop Garden of Life® RAW vanilla spiced chai protein

½ tsp. pumpkin pie spice

Blend all ingredients until smooth

Nutrition Facts
280 calories, 43g carbohydrates, 20g protein

*Training Tip
Whether you're training for a PR (personal record) in the 5k or the marathon, it's a good idea to set your sights on that goal at least 12-18 weeks in advance in order to train adequately. Though you can't control things like race day weather, you certainly can control your diet and training. As you continue to get faster, PRs will become more difficult to achieve and require attention to detail. Keeping a running log will also help you review what you did for your last PR and give you an idea of what needs to be tweaked in your next training cycle.

Chiango Cool-Down

Chia seeds have been a popular topic of conversation with runners over the last several years, and for good reason. This little seed is packed with all kinds of nutrition including hefty amounts of protein and dietary fiber that our bodies can immediately use. As you'll see, they also add a great texture to any smoothie. This refreshing recipe is one that could easily be consumed as fuel before a run or after a run for recovery.

Ingredients
1 cup cold coconut water (VitaCoco® Peach & Mango flavor – optional)
½ fresh large mango (peeled & pitted)

Juice of 1 lime
2 Tbsp. chia seeds
2-3 ice cubes

Blend all ingredients until smooth

Nutrition Facts
318 calories, 59g carbohydrates, 6.6g protein, 14.4g dietary fiber

*Training Tip
Similar to a warm-up, a cool down is essential after a hard workout or race in order to loosen muscles and help rid the body of lactic acid. I generally like to do a solid 1-2 miles of very easy running post-race or workout. A cool down will allow your next run to feel even better!

Giddy Up Granny

Most of us are familiar with the phrase, 'an apple a day, keeps the doctor away.' Apples are a great source of dietary fiber which helps bind up waste throughout the body. Not only do they contain plenty of antioxidants but Granny Smith apples are slightly higher in potassium than other varieties. By the way, eat the skin (only if organic) also since it contains a high amount of vitamin content.

Ingredients
1 cup cold water
½ Granny Smith apple
⅓ cup frozen pineapple chunks
Small handful raw baby spinach
1 squeezed lemon wedge or 1 tsp. lemon juice

1 scoop Garden of Life® Smooth Vanilla Organic Plant Protein

Blend all ingredients until smooth

Nutrition Facts
162 calories, 28.4g carbohydrates, 16.8g protein, 8.4g dietary fiber

*Training Tip
Looking to cut a few unwanted pounds? This smoothie recipe will only encourage any goals you have in this area with its lower calorie, yet high nutrient content. Speaking of dropping a few pounds, try doing several runs a week first thing in the morning after waking up. This will encourage your body to burn fat as fuel rather than utilizing the food you ate earlier. I do recommend drinking 12 ounces of water every morning upon waking in order to help jumpstart your metabolism. One other tip is to refrain from eating anything (except water) after 7pm each evening. If you get a slight hunger pain after that, just remind yourself that nothing worth having comes without a little pain involved.

Nut Butter Splurge

Apples or bananas dipped in nut butter are a delicious and healthy snack. In this recipe, you get the benefit of both! You'll be giving your body the opportunity to splurge on some healthy fats which can serve as a nice slow-burning fuel for a longer run or a protein packed recovery smoothie. No need to feel guilty with this delicious blend.

Ingredients

1 cup unsweetened almond milk
1 Tbsp. almond butter
1 Tbsp. peanut butter
½ frozen banana
1 red delicious apple

1 scoop Garden of Life® Smooth Almond Butter Organic Plant Protein

Blend all ingredients until smooth

Nutrition Facts
464 calories, 24.4g protein, 41g carbohydrates, 21.9g fat, 10.5g dietary fiber

*Training Tip
Sometimes my body will give me signs that it's crying out for calories. On occasion, when this happens, I will sometimes help myself to a heaping spoonful of peanut or almond butter. This immediately provides a quick 100-150 calories along with 3-5 grams of protein and 7-9 grams of fat. Though I don't recommend camping out by the jar of peanut butter, doing this every now and then will help stave off a mild hunger pain, especially during periods of more intense training.

Carrot Cake Cruise

If you like carrot cake, you're going to enjoy this delicious healthy alternative. Carrots are most often thought of as a source of the carotenoid beta-carotene. They're also full of many other phytonutrient antioxidants which help fight cancer cells and guard against artery damage. Carrots are also high in vitamin A. With the raisins and rice milk, this recipe might also remind you of rice or carrot pudding.

Ingredients

1 cup plain rice milk

1 large carrot

½ frozen ripe banana

1 Medjool date, soaked & pitted

2 Tbsp. raisins
½ tsp. vanilla
½ tsp. cinnamon
½ tsp. all spice

Blend all ingredients until smooth

Nutrition Facts
359 calories, 84g carbohydrates, 6g dietary fiber

*Training Tip
Speaking of 'cruise', you may have heard the term cruise intervals. These are intervals of 3-10 minutes of running at about 15 seconds slower than your 10k pace. So if your 10k pace is 6 minutes per mile (37:12 10k), you would run at 6:15 pace for no more than 10 minutes at a time before taking a short recovery period. A cruise interval workout might include 3-4 of these segments throughout the run.

Passion Fruit Pick-Up

This smoothie is one you're sure to become 'passionate' about. Depending on where you live, you may not always have passion fruit available in your grocery stores. When you do, grab them while you can. This small, tasty tropical fruit provides several health benefits including asthma relief, keeping skin hydrated & glowing, and boosting immunity with ample amounts of vitamin C and vitamin A. Brazil nuts are a nice compliment to passion fruit and are a powerhouse for nutrition including muscle growth and repair with the protein and healthy fat content. Brazil nuts are a very satisfying snack that can easily curb cravings (just 6 nuts = 200 calories).

Ingredients
1 cup cold coconut water
Insides of 3 passion fruit including seeds*
3 brazil nuts

2 Tbsp. shredded coconut

1 Tbsp. honey

3-4 ice cubes

*Preparation Tip: Here's a helpful link for preparing and eating passion fruit - http://www.wikihow.com/Eat-Passionfruit

Blend all ingredients until smooth

Nutrition Facts

360 calories, 6.1g protein, 44.3g carbohydrates, 11.5g dietary fiber

*Training Tip

When you hear the term 'pick-up' within the running community, it simply refers to an acceleration done within a run. Unlike a fartlek, pick-ups last no more than thirty seconds at most. It's just another way you can spice up a scheduled easy run no matter what the terrain. In a race situation, pick-ups are a great way to test those around you to see if they'll go with you. If they don't, you've opened a small gap that they may not be able to cover. This could also be referred to as a 'surge.'

Chocolacado Chiller

You're in for a treat with this smoothie...emphasis on 'smooth!' Though it's packed with a few more calories, this recipe is also packed with plenty of protein, carbs, good fat and fiber. Ideal as either fuel for a longer run (90 minutes or more) or post long run recovery, you'll be giving your body quality nutrition no matter what. Cacao has long been known as a 'superfood' that's packed with antioxidants (20 times more than blueberries!). The Incas considered it a 'drink of gods' when raw cacao was added. Enjoy this more indulgent recipe without shame!

Ingredients

1 cup coconut milk

½ ripe avocado

2 soaked & pitted Medjool dates

2 Tbsp. cacao powder

1 Tbsp. ground flax seed
1 scoop Garden of Life® Smooth Chocolate Organic Plant Protein
2 ice cubes

Blend all ingredients until smooth

Nutrition Facts
525 calories, 21.1g protein, 58.5g carbohydrates, 25g fat, 16.6g dietary fiber

*Training Tip
Speaking of 'chiller', some of us live in places that get downright cold in the winter. If you have access to a treadmill, it's not a bad option on days when you'd rather not deal with frigid temperatures or possibly have a workout you aren't able to complete outdoors due to snow & ice. One of my favorite things to do on a treadmill is a mild, progressive tempo run. I immediately set the grade at 1% to make up for some wind I might have faced outside. Beginning at 6.1 or 9:50 pace, I then increase the speed one notch every 2 minutes until I reach the 30 minute mark where I then increase the speed one notch every minute until I hit the 50 minute mark. From there, I go into a 20 minute cool down starting at 8:00 pace (7.5) and slowing down one notch every 2 minutes. Try this type of run sometime at a pace that suits you personally. A 70 minute run with lots of variety!

Green hemoGoblin

Unlike the Green Goblin in Spider-Man, this smoothie is any-thing but a villain. In fact, it's a hemoglobin hero! Spinach, kale and broccoli are all rich in folate, a B complex vitamin that plays a crucial role in helping to build red blood cells in the body. When our bodies are low in folate, our running will suffer in numerous ways, including fatigue, weak immunity and a foggy brain. I suggest working this lean smoothie into your weekly routine at least 1-2 times.

Ingredients
½ cup cold unsweetened apple juice
½ cup cold water
½ frozen banana
Small handful raw spinach
1 cup chopped kale (stem included)
½ cup raw broccoli

1 scoop Garden of Life® Perfect Food green powder (chlorella or wheat grass powder is another option)

Blend all ingredients until smooth

Nutrition Facts
201 calories, 40.9g carbohydrates, 8.7g protein, 7.2g dietary fiber

*Training Tip
Have you ever experienced periods of fatigue or a lack of power in your running? How about feeling absent-minded or just foggy in the head? These are possible signs that your body may be low in iron or B vitamins, including folate. It's always a good idea to get a blood test to see where your various levels are and what might be low. Specifically, have them check your hemoglobin, ferritin and vitamin B12 for any possible deficiencies.

RhuBerry Ride

In the backyard of the house where I grew up, we had a hearty rhubarb patch that lasted many years before it finally died out. On occasion, my dad would go out and cut a couple stalks which would be used for a strawberry-rhubarb cobbler made by my mom. This smoothie is a variation of that child-hood memory with just the right amount of sweet and tart. Rhubarb is high in vitamin K which plays a significant role in brain health, including delaying or even preventing the onset of Alzheimer's disease. Vitamin K also helps stimulate bone growth and repair, a nice benefit for runners.

Ingredients
1 cup unsweetened almond milk
¾ cup chopped rhubarb stalk (don't eat the toxic leaves)
½ cup frozen strawberries

1 Tbsp. honey

1 Tbsp. oats

Pinch of cinnamon

1 scoop Garden of Life® Smooth Vanilla Organic Plant Protein

Blend all ingredients until smooth

Nutrition Facts

306 calories, 39g carbohydrates, 19.4g protein, 8.5g dietary fiber

*Training Tip

When it comes to 'ride', you don't want to mess around with shoes that don't fit your feet properly. I recommend going to your nearest specialty running store to get a proper analysis of your gait and stride. Each person is a little different in terms of what they need and a running store specialist can identify things that others can't through experience. Taking a pair of shoes out for a test drive around the parking lot is a good idea before making the purchase.

Sweet & Spicy Shakeout

Serrano (chili) peppers contain a substance called capsaicin which has been shown to help reduce inflammation. This is also the substance that accounts for the spicy, pungent flavor. Hot peppers of all varieties also aid in circulation throughout the body. Feeling a little stuffed up in the nose? Nothing like a pepper to open up the sinuses! When you add the antioxidant boost of blackberries, this recipe offers a unique 1-2 punch of health benefits.

Ingredients

1 cup coconut milk

1 cup frozen blackberries

1 fresh serrano pepper (seeds optional)

½ cup plain Greek yogurt or non-dairy alternative (i.e. So Delicious®)

1 Tbsp. Agave nectar
1 Tsp. lemon juice (or juice of 1 wedge)

Blend all ingredients until smooth

Nutrition Facts
239 calories, 40.5g carbohydrates, 8.2g protein, 10g dietary fiber

*Training Tip
One of the "secrets" I've learned that many elite level runners practice is something called the pre-race shakeout run. What this does is wake up the body and loosens up the legs ahead of time. It also prepares the digestive system for the pre-race meal. About 3-3 ½ hours before race start, roll out of bed and drink about 8 ounces of water, put on the running shoes and head out the door for a very easy 10 minute run. Upon returning, do some light stretching and then proceed to eat your pre-race meal. By the time you get to your pre-race warm-up (about 30-40 minutes before race start), you'll be looser and feeling a little more prepared to race.

Salted Caramel Cashew Carb Load

With over a hundred grams of carbs, you don't want to partake of this smoothie on a daily basis. I recommend trying this one as pre-long run fuel by getting it into your body 3-3.5 hours before starting the run. It should easily sustain you through over 2 hours of running. The high fiber in dates offers a nice even sugar release into the bloodstream which is perfect in longer efforts. The fat content of the cashew butter offers an additional fuel source ideal for long runs. And it's always good to take in a little extra salt before longer runs to make up for what is lost through sweat.

Ingredients

1 cup cashew milk (i.e. Silk® brand)

4 soaked & pitted Medjool dates

1 Tbsp. cashew butter (or 10-12 whole cashews)

1 Tsp. vanilla extract
1 Tbsp. honey
Pinch of sea salt
2-3 ice cubes

Blend all ingredients until smooth

Nutrition Facts
494 calories, 5g protein, 103g carbohydrates, 10.4g fat, 6.7g dietary fiber

*Training Tip
Carbo-loading is a practice that has been around for decades. The idea is to deliberately restrict carb intake in the week leading up to a long run or race (such as a marathon) and then load up on carbs in the 1-2 days before the run or race in order for glycogen stores in the muscles (main source of fuel) to be topped off and available for immediate use. Though I'm not a big fan of carbo-loading in this traditional sense, many runners have benefitted from this technique. My philosophy is simply to eat a variety of nutrients and then eat a sensible carb-heavy meal the night before the race without overeating. After all, you don't want to be carrying any unnecessary weight on race day by overindulging in the 1-2 days pre-race.

Apricot Afterburner

Apricots are a good source of catechins which are in the family of flavonoid phytonutrients. These catechins are potent anti-inflammatory nutrients. They're also rich in carotenoids which help protect eyesight from age-related damage. This lean recipe is a good choice for those of you looking to shed a few unnecessary pounds and still add a nice dose of nutrition.

Ingredients
1 cup vanilla coconut milk
3 fresh pitted apricots
1 scoop Garden of Life® Smooth Vanilla Organic Plant Protein
Pinch of cinnamon
2 ice cubes

Blend all ingredients until smooth

Nutrition Facts
242 calories, 16.5g protein, 28g carbohydrates, 6.1g dietary fiber

*Training Tip
Interestingly enough, numerous studies have shown that many runners actually tend to gain weight despite the myriad of other health benefits this simple sport offers. The biggest reason is that most runners tend to run day after day at the same pace. By setting aside a couple days a week for higher intensity intervals, runners can increase their metabolism which will create an 'afterburner' affect post workout. In other words, your body will burn more calories. I personally like to set aside Tuesdays for either an interval or fartlek workout and Fridays for tempo runs. An example of a Tuesday workout might be 12 x 400 meters on the track at goal 5k race pace with a 200-400 meter jog rest between each fast rep. Another might be a fartlek run where I simply throw in several segments of 30-60 seconds of really hard running with the same amount of jog rest on a routine run on the road or trail. For a Friday tempo, I like to run for 20-25 minutes at 30-40 seconds slower than 5k race pace per mile. By significantly increasing the heart rate a couple times each week, you'll be on your way to creating the ideal conditions for higher calorie burn and increased metabolism.

Matcha Macho Man

For those of you looking for an energy boost, this is your recipe. Matcha green tea powder has been shown to boost metabolism, enhance mood, aid in concentration, lower cholesterol and blood sugar. It's also rich in chlorophyll as evidenced in its green color. Matcha is also an absolute powerhouse for antioxidants, surpassing (by far) goji berries, pomegranate, blueberries, acai berries, broccoli and spinach. Now that's something even the Village People can sing about.

Ingredients
1 cup chilled green tea
1 scoop Garden of Life® Vanilla Spiced Chai Raw Protein
1 frozen banana

1 Tsp. matcha green tea powder

Pinch of cinnamon

Pinch of cardamom

Blend all ingredients until smooth

Nutrition Facts

212 calories, 32g carbohydrates, 20.5g protein, 6.1g dietary fiber, 85mg caffeine

*Training Tip

Speaking of 'macho', runners can certainly benefit from a weekly strength training routine in order to prevent muscle imbalances and overuse injuries. I few that I like are body-weight squats, single leg squats, push-ups and some core work that includes planks. Here's an article that can whet the appetite and help point you in the right direction: http://running.competitor.com/2014/08/training/the-four-best-strength-training-exercises-for-runners_40725

Conclusion

We've come to the end of this smoothie journey. 24 delicious and nutritious stops along the way and our bodies are better for it. But the journey doesn't need to end here. I've merely provided some fresh ideas to zest up your smoothie rotation.

Now it's your turn.

I want to encourage you to experiment with numerous ingredients in your blender. Some recipes are going to be keepers and some are going to 'one and done' concoctions. There's no harm in trying something new and unique, even if you decide that recipe isn't going to make the cut. Eventually, you're going to discover some real winners as you become bold and daring with what you throw together!

When you discover those 'winners', share those recipes with friends, family and your social media following. We're all looking for fun ways to put good things into our bodies. You just might become known as a local 'Smoothie King or Queen.'

Thanks for taking the time to try some of these recipes. I would so appreciate it if you'd consider stopping by my Amazon book page to share a review.

Until we meet again, here's to a healthy and vibrant life...Cheers!

www.TrainWellRaceWell.com

Interested in Receiving Coaching?

CJ coaches runners of all levels both locally and online. He's a USATF Level 1 Certified running coach who has a passion to help you achieve your running goals and maximize your full potential. CJ would love to work with you and provide some accountability in your training and nutrition.

Check out his coaching services here:

http://www.trainwellracewell.com/private-coaching/

Thank you to some great sponsors...

Garden of Life - www.GardenOfLife.com

BeetElite beet juice powder - www.BeetElite.com

BodyHealth - www.BodyHealth.com

Freedom Chiropractic - www.FreedomChiro.com

Your nearest Maximized Living Chiropractor:
www.MaximizedLiving.com

Brooks Running – www.BrooksRunning.com

Honey Stinger – www.HoneyStinger.com

Train Well Race Well - www.TrainWellRaceWell.com

Vitamix - www.vitamix.com (The only blender I'll ever use)

Contact

I'd love to hear from you! Which smoothie recipe is your favorite from this book? What variations worked best for you? Contact me here:

http://www.trainwellracewell.com/contact/.

I look forward to hearing from you!

You can also connect with me at:

www.facebook.com/runningtipsandadvice

or

www.twitter.com/cjhitz

Here's to many great runs ahead,
CJ

CJ Hitz, author of the "Eat to Run" series

Photo by Tim Bergsten/Pikespeaksports.us

Who is CJ?

After running in the 1988 State Cross Country meet in Eugene, Oregon as a high school sophomore, CJ gave up running for nearly 20 years before being drawn back into the sport.

CJ caught the "running bug" in 2008 and has not looked back since. He's dropped over 50 pounds in weight and continues to set new lifetime personal bests as a national class masters runner. CJ has competed in well over 150 races ranging from road 5Ks to trail 50Ks. He enjoys a fast road 5k or a grueling mountain race with lots of elevation gain & loss. Basically, he just plain loves running.

CJ and his wife Shelley reside in Colorado Springs, CO where they are spoiled beyond measure with mountains, trails and sunshine.

Oh...and he's also a HUGE fan of smoothies!

"Dear friend, I pray that you may enjoy good health and that all may go well with you, even as your soul is getting along well." - 3 John 1:2

If you haven't had a chance to check out CJ's first Smoothies For Runners book where you'll find 32 more smoothie recipes, you can find it here:

http://smarturl.it/smoothiesforrunners

Made in the
USA
Monee, IL